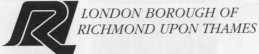

D0294316

Written by: Goh Sui Noi and Lim Bee Ling
Editors: Cheryl Sim and Melvin Neo
Designer: Benson Tan
Photo research: Thomas Khoo

PHOTO CREDITS

Alamy/Bes Stock: 6, 11, 15 (bottom), 25, 29, 38 (bottom), 41
Bes Stock: 4, 5, 7
Dave G. Houser: 38 (top), 40
Focus Team–Italy: 23
Getty Images: 14, 26, 30 (top), 37
Graham Uden: 22
Hutchison Library: cover, 1, 2, 9 (top), 10 (top), 12, 20, 21, 24, 32 (top), 33
Photolibrary: 3 (bottom), 16, 19, 31, 32 (bottom), 34, 35
Richard I'Anson: 18
Topham Picturepoint: 3 (top), 10 (bottom), 15 (top and centre), 27, 30 (bottom), 36, 45
Trip Photographic Library: 8, 13, 17, 28, 39
Yu Hui Ying: 3 (centre), 9 (bottom)

This edition published in 2010
by Franklin Watts

Designed and originated by
Marshall Cavendish International (Asia) Pte Ltd
Copyright © Marshall Cavendish International (Asia) Pte Ltd 2010
Marshall Cavendish is a trademark of Times Publishing Limited.

Franklin Watts
338 Euston Road
London NW1 3BH

This publication represents the opinions and views of the authors
based on their personal experience, knowledge and research. The
information in this book serves as a general guide only. The authors
and publisher have used their best efforts in preparing this book
and disclaim liability rising directly and indirectly from the use and
application of this book.

Dewey number 951'.06

ISBN 978 1 4451 0198 9

Franklin Watts is a division of Hachette Children's Books,
an Hachette UK company.
www.hachette.co.uk

Printed in Malaysia

Contents

Words that appear in the glossary are printed in **boldface** type the first time they occur in the text.

In China, many people own bicycles as it is an inexpensive and convenient means of transportation.

Welcome to China!

More than 1.3 billion people live in China. This means that one in every five people in the world is Chinese! China is an ancient country. Despite its long and troubled past, it enjoys peace and prosperity today. Let's meet the Chinese people and visit their country, the 'Land of the Dragon'.

Located in Beijing, the Forbidden City consists of palaces where China's emperors once lived.

The Flag of China

The Chinese flag has five yellow stars on a red background. The stars represent the government and the Chinese people. The colour red symbolizes **revolution**.

The Land

Located in East Asia, China is the third largest country in the world, after Russia and Canada. It has a land area of 9.6 million square kilometres. Most of the land consists of mountains and **plateaus**. The tallest peak on Earth, Mt. Everest, or Zhumulangma Feng to the Chinese, sits on the border between China and Nepal.

A narrow dirt road winds through the Ganjia grassland area of Gansu province, in central China.

China's Yunnan province boasts beautiful, snowcapped mountains.

Plains make up eastern China. **Arid** deserts stretch across western and northern China.

Many people live along China's two longest rivers, the Yangtze, or 'Long River', and the Huanghe, more commonly known throughout the world as the 'Yellow River'. The Yangtze is the third longest river in the world. The Yellow River is also called 'China's Sorrow'. It causes great destruction when it overflows its banks during the **monsoon** season, which falls between the months of May and October.

Seasons

China's weather conditions vary greatly because of its size. Northeastern China experiences bitterly cold winters with temperatures as low as −8° Celsius. Southern China, however, remains warm all year round. In the southeastern provinces, the climate is warm and humid. People living on the Qinghai-Tibet Plateau in western China experience cold, but sunny, weather.

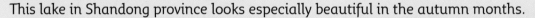

This lake in Shandong province looks especially beautiful in the autumn months.

Jiuzaigou in northern Sichuan is famous for its spectacular waterfalls.

Plants and Animals

China is home to many kinds of tree, such as oak, maple, pine and China cypress. Flowering plants that grow there include peonies and chrysanthemums. China also provides a home for many unique animals, including the rare golden monkey.

The giant panda lives in the mountain areas of central China. Today, pandas face extinction because the bamboo forests that provide their only food source are shrinking.

The red bear cat, a type of panda, lives in the forests bordering Tibet and India.

History

Early History

About 500,000 years ago, **primitive** humans lived in caves in China. About seven thousand years ago, the first villages, made of earth and wood, appeared along the Yellow River.

During the Shang dynasty, people learnt how to make bronze objects. They carved records of their daily lives on some of these objects.

The First Dynasties

Ancient China was ruled by kings. Each **dynasty**, or line of kings, ruled until another conquered it. The earliest Chinese kingdoms were the Xia, Shang and Zhou dynasties.

The Zhou king divided his land into territories under the control of dukes and princes. From 770 to 476 BCE, however, many territories fought against each other for land and power. After many years of war, only seven states survived. **Confucius**, China's famous **philosopher** and teacher, lived during this warring period.

A boy practises brush painting, the ancient Chinese art of writing.

Centuries ago, the Silk Road was a trading route connecting China and the West. Today, the Silk Road is still in use, winding through deserts and mountains.

Two hundred years later, the Qin king defeated all the other states and united China. He called himself Qin Shihuang (CHIN shih-huang), or 'First Emperor'.

The Chinese invented paper and printing. When new land and sea routes were discovered, China began to trade with the rest of the world.

The Great Wall of China runs for thousands of miles across China's vast landscape. Signal towers were built on hilltops and used as a means of communicating with soldiers stationed along the wall.

Qin Shihuang and the Great Wall

China's first emperor, Qin Shihuang, wanted to protect his country from invaders from the north. In 214 BCE, the walls dividing one territory from another were connected to make one long wall, the Great Wall of China.

Empress Wu Zetian (625-704)

China's only female ruler was Empress Wu Zetian. At first, she ruled through her son, the emperor, but in 690, she took the throne herself. China prospered under her leadership.

The Opium Wars

In the 1800s, Britain and China were fighting to gain more control over the sale and supply of **opium**. This erupted into two major battles over trade, which came to be known as the Opium Wars. After China's defeat, its people grew unhappy with the government for failing to protect the country's interests, and for Hong Kong's fall into British hands. By the early twentieth century, the Qing dynasty, which had ruled China for more than two hundred years, had lost much of its power and popularity.

Political Struggle

When the Qing dynasty fell in 1911, the Nationalist Party of China, or the Kuomintang, established the **Republic** of China. Dr. Sun Yat-sen, a Western-educated medical doctor, became China's first president.

However, Sun† could not bring peace to the new nation. Army generals fought among themselves for power. China also suffered losses when Japan attacked the city of Nanjing in 1937.

† In Chinese culture, the family name is written before the person's given name.

Chiang Kai-shek, a colleague of Sun Yat-sen, helped Sun defeat the warring army generals after the Republic of China was established. After Sun's death in 1925, Chiang became the leader of the Kuomintang.

Opponents of the Kuomintang formed the Chinese Communist Party in 1921. After World War II, the **Communists**, led by Mao Zedong, defeated the Kuomintang in 1949 and founded the People's Republic of China. Mao's two programmes, The Great Leap Forward and the Cultural Revolution, were unsuccessful and caused much suffering and hardship. A widespread famine resulted in many deaths and innocent citizens were harshly punished for having personal wealth. After Mao died in 1976, Deng Xiaoping became the leader of the Communist Party. Deng introduced many economic changes to **modernize** China.

On 1 October 1949, China and the rest of the world listened as Mao Zedong announced the founding of the People's Republic of China at Tiananmen Square in Beijing.

Sun Yat-sen (1866–1925)

Sun became the Republic's first president when the Qing dynasty collapsed in 1911. He is regarded as the 'Father of Modern China'.

Dr. Sun Yat-sen

Mao Zedong (1893–1976)

Mao became the leader of the People's Republic of China in 1949. He rebuilt China by constructing factories, railways and roads. However, his other programmes, namely The Great Leap Forward and the Cultural Revolution, greatly damaged the economy.

Mao Zedong

Deng Xiaoping (1904–1997)

Deng, a member of the Communist Party, tried to solve China's economic problems in the 1960s. Government officials reduced Deng's power because he disagreed with some of their policies. After Mao died in 1976, Deng regained power. His programmes improved the lives of the Chinese.

Deng Xiaoping

The Government and the Economy

The Communist Party of China

China is governed by the Communist Party of China. The president, Hu Jintao, is the head of state.

The National People's Congress elects the president and vice president. Every five years, the Chinese people choose members of the Congress from throughout China.

Every president of the People's Republic of China can serve a maximum of two terms, each lasting five years. Current president Hu Jintao's second term will end in 2013.

These children attend school in Sichuan province. The State Council is in charge of health and education.

The State Council

China consists of thirty-one provinces, autonomous regions and **municipalities**. Each of them has a government that reports to the State Council. The State Council is a governmental agency headed by the prime minister. Its responsibilities include building schools and training doctors and nurses. China's armed forces, police and courts **enforce** law and order.

Economy

China consists mainly of deserts and mountains. Only one-tenth of the land is suitable for growing crops. Nevertheless, farmers make up more than 70 per cent of China's population. In the drier, northern part of the country, farmers grow crops, such as wheat and corn, that can survive without much water. In the warmer, wetter regions of the south, rice is the main crop.

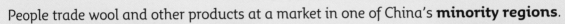

People trade wool and other products at a market in one of China's **minority regions**.

The Three Gorges Dam on the Yangtze River is the world's biggest human-made dam and the single largest generator of electricity. It took nearly fourteen years to be built.

Most of China's electricity is produced from coal. China also mines iron, oil and tin. These resources allow China to manufacture its own aeroplanes, ships, cars and various other machines.

To gain an additional source of electricity—and to control floods during monsoon seasons—China built the world's largest dam, the Three Gorges Dam. Modern railways and roads transport people and goods between major cities.

People and Lifestyle

Han Chinese are the largest of the fifty-six ethnic groups in China. They make up about 92 per cent of the population. They live mainly along the Yellow and Yangtze rivers and in the northeastern regions. Government policy does not allow Han couples in cities to have more than one child. This is to avoid problems of overcrowding and lack of food.

The government introduced the one-child policy in the 1980s. Today, most urban couples have only one child.

In Kazakh culture, it is common for large and extended families to live together under one roof.

Ethnic Minorities

Most of China's minorities live close to the country's borders. They have their own customs, languages and beliefs. Kazakhs and Mongolians live in the northern grasslands. They move with their cattle in search of pasture. Most Mongolians are Buddhists while the Kazakhs are Muslims. The Tibetans in southwestern China are farmers or cattle herders. Other ethnic minorities include the Dai, Hui, Li, Uighurs and Zhuangs.

Family Life

For centuries, the teachings of Confucius have influenced the Chinese. They believe that a strong family is the basis of a good society. Everyone is expected to respect and obey their elders. Some Chinese favour sons over daughters because sons carry on the family name and are expected to look after the parents in old age. Confucius also placed great emphasis on education and the arts.

In a traditional Chinese family, the elderly live with a son and help take care of their grandchildren.

This Chinese woman sells handmade crafts, clothing and embroidery to earn additional income for her family.

Getting Married

In the past, parents chose marriage partners for their children. Today, many young people are free to choose their own partners. In a traditional wedding ceremony, the bride and groom kneel before their elders and offer them tea to show their respect. Then, the couple join family and friends in a lunch or dinner celebration.

Education

From the age of six, children attend classes between 8 a.m. and 5 p.m. six days a week. Chinese students study many subjects, including history, geography, literature, mathematics, music and science.

In the countryside and in poor areas, there are few schools. A child may have to travel long distances to get to school in these areas.

Despite living in the country, these young children are lucky enough to attend school. At least one meal is eaten in school before the children make the long journey back home.

Students in China are skilled on the computer.

After completing six years of primary education, students can go on to attend six years of secondary school. If they wish to study at a university, they must first pass a national exam.

Since the People's Republic of China was founded, the Chinese Communist Party has made education available to everyone. Adult education was introduced to teach older people who may have missed out when they were young. Today, more than 75 per cent of China's adult population can read and write.

Taoism and Buddhism

The most popular religions in China are Taoism and Buddhism. Taoism is an ancient set of beliefs that teaches people to live in harmony with nature. Chinese Buddhism combines Taoism with other Chinese beliefs and with Indian Buddhism.

A monk makes his offerings at a Taoist temple in Xiamen.

The Hui minority group is Muslim. Many Hui people visit this mosque near the Yellow River.

Many Chinese believe in gods and nature spirits. They also believe that when a person dies, he or she goes to another world. Family members burn special paper houses, paper cars and money for the dead. They also place food at the graves.

Islam and Christianity

Ethnic minorities such as the Kazakhs and Huis are Muslims. Small groups of Christians live in cities such as Beijing and Shanghai.

Language

A Mixed Language

The Han Chinese speak many **dialects**, but everyone learns a language called Mandarin. It is also known as *putonghua* (PU-TONG-hua), or 'the common language'.

All Chinese dialects share one written form. There is no alphabet. Words consist of characters that look like drawings.

This streetside reading stand allows people to borrow books and read them on the spot for a small fee. Comic books are popular as they can be read quickly in one sitting.

Mandarin characters are displayed on a street wall.

Literature

The earliest Chinese poems date back to about 600 BCE. Many **classical** poems by great poets such as Li Sao are still read and enjoyed today. Drama developed during the Yuan dynasty (1206–1368). The first Chinese novels appeared during the Ming dynasty (1368–1644). Chinese legends and folk tales have been handed down for centuries.

Arts

Some of China's traditional art forms are thousands of years old. **Calligraphy** and brush painting survived difficult periods in China's history when the arts were strictly controlled. Today, many Chinese painters blend traditional brush painting with Western styles. They paint human figures, landscapes, flowers and animals on silk or paper.

This vase is being handpainted.

Many Chinese paintings feature graceful, yet powerful, animals, such as tigers.

An opera actor performs in a colourful warrior costume.

Chinese Opera

Still popular today, Chinese opera began about nine hundred years ago. The actors wear bright costumes and paint their faces so audiences can recognize their characters easily.

A traditional music group performs in Yunnan.

Music

On important occasions, such as weddings and funerals, Chinese musicians perform with traditional instruments, such as the flute, **zither** and drums.

Film

The first Chinese films were made in the 1920s. Many Chinese actors and directors, such as Ang Lee, win international awards today.

Gong Li is one of China's most popular actors.

Folk Crafts

Many Chinese practise folk crafts, such as **embroidery** and paper-cutting. During festive seasons, homes are decorated with paper designs. Red is a very popular colour during Chinese New Year. The Chinese believe it symbolizes good luck.

This young girl is stitching a colourful design following the ancient Chinese art of embroidery.

Leisure Time

In the past, many Chinese were too poor to enjoy much free time. Today, however, they look forward to a variety of leisure activities. People in cities watch television, go to the cinema and eat at restaurants. In the countryside, people who cannot afford television sets play traditional card games. Some children invent their own games.

In the evenings, many couples enjoy ballroom dancing on pavements and in open spaces.

Card games are a favourite pastime among the older generation.

While dance clubs and bowling alleys attract many young people, the older generation still prefers to gather in parks for ballroom dancing, chess, reading the papers or to chat with friends. Bird owners also bring their songbirds to the parks to compare their singing skills with other birds.

When they are not studying, children enjoy playing their favourite games such as skipping and hide-and-seek.

Sports

As early as 5 a.m., people begin to assemble in the parks for morning exercises.

Traditional exercises, such as *taijiquan* (TAI-chi-CHUAN), or shadowboxing, involve deep breathing to strengthen the body. *Wushu* (WU-shu), or *gongfu* (GONG-foo), involves hand **combat** or fighting with weapons.

Many Chinese perform *taijiquan* outdoors early in the morning.

China's male table tennis players celebrate on home turf at the 2008 Olympics in Beijing after winning the gold, silver and bronze medals in the men's singles matches.

Popular sports include basketball, table tennis, swimming and badminton. To promote sports, the government provides sports facilities in factories, schools, and government buildings.

China has achieved outstanding results in many international sports competitions, including the Olympic Games. Its national team excels in gymnastics, track and field, badminton, swimming and diving.

Festivals

Chinese people throughout the world celebrate Chinese New Year. Weeks before the festival, every household cleans the house and decorates it with red paper-cuttings. On Chinese New Year's Eve, family members get together for a **reunion** dinner. Children love the festival because they receive *hongbao* (HOHNG-pao), or red packets containing money!

Tangerine trees are decorated for Chinese New Year.

New Year celebrations include traditional performances by **stilt-walkers**.

Tomb-Sweeping Day

On 5 April, families visit the burial grounds of their ancestors. They sweep the tombs clean to show respect for the dead.

Dragon Boat Festival

On this day, the Chinese race in dragon boats and eat rice dumplings. This ritual which is usually held in May is in memory of Qu Yuan (340–278 BCE), a poet who lived during the Warring States period.

The Dai people in Yunnan province drench each other with waterguns during a New Year festival.

Mid-Autumn Festival

During this festival which is celebrated in late September or early October, the Chinese gather to admire the full harvest moon and eat **moon cakes**. At night, children carry candle-lit lanterns.

Minority Festivals

Ethnic minorities have their own festivals. The Dai people in Yunnan province splash water on each other in the spring during the New Year festival to wash away bad luck.

Food

The Chinese people celebrate special occasions with all kinds of delicious food, from dumplings to suckling pig.

   A typical Chinese meal, however, is simple. It consists of vegetables, rice, soup and meat. The Chinese also love to drink tea. In fact, tea drinking began in China about five thousand years ago.

Many kinds of food are available in China. Meals are so important to the Chinese that they greet each other by asking, "Have you eaten?".

A child grabs a quick bite at one of China's numerous open-air snack stalls.

Western China, especially the Sichuan province, is known for its spicy food cooked with plenty of chillies. In the eastern regions, people enjoy fresh seafood, such as shellfish and fish, eaten with rice. Northerners in and around Beijing use a lot of chillies and garlic in their food. In the southern part of the country, food is lightly seasoned to bring out its full flavour. China's minority groups have their own unique dishes.

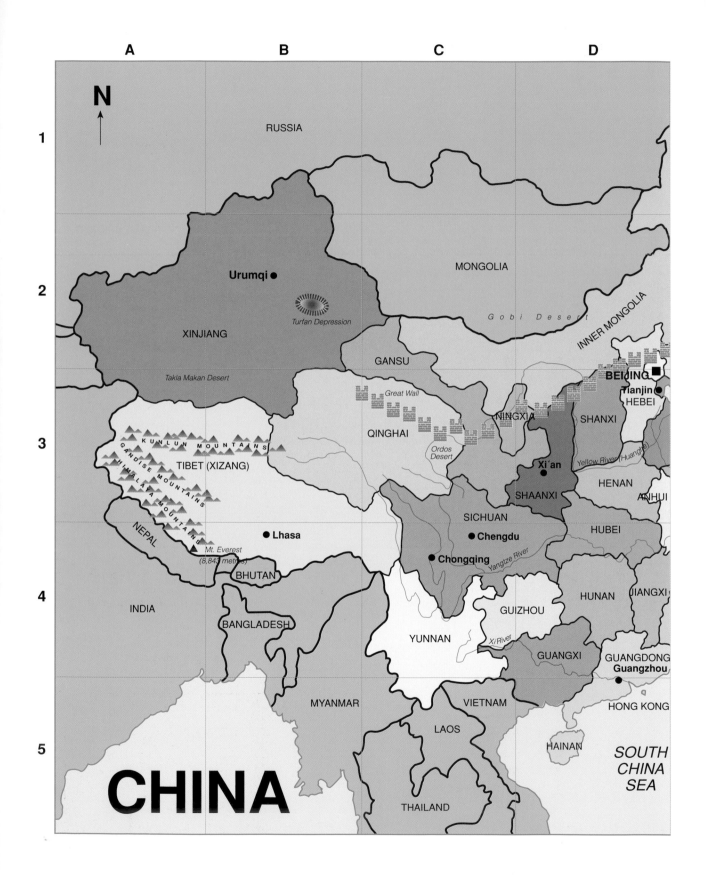

Anhui D3

Bangladesh B4
Beijing D3
Bhutan B4
Bohai E3

Chengdu C4
Chongqing C4

East China Sea E3
Everest, Mt. A4

Fujian E4

Gansu C2
Gobi Desert C2–D2
Grand Canal E3
Great Wall C3
Guangdong D4
Guangxi D4
Guangzhou D4
Guizhou C4

Hainan D5
Hebei D3
Heilongjiang E2
Henan D3
Himalaya Mountains A3
Hong Kong D5
Hubei D4
Hunan D4

India A4
Inner Mongolia D2

Japan F3
Jiangsu E3
Jiangxi D4
Jilin E2

Kunlun Mountains A3

Laos C5
Lhasa B4
Liaoning E2

Mongolia C2
Myanmar B5

Nanjing E3
Nepal A4
Ningxia C3
North Korea E2

Ordos Desert C3

Qinghai C3

Russia B1

Sea of Japan F2
Shaanxi D3
Shandong E3
Shanghai E4
Shanxi D3
Sichuan C3
South China Sea D5
South Korea E3

Taiwan E4
Takla Makan Desert
  A3–B3
Thailand C5
Tianjin D3
Tibet (Xizang) B3
Turfan Depression B2

Vietnam C5

Xi River C4
Xiamen E4
Xi'an D3
Xinjiang A2

Yangtze River B3-E3
Yellow Sea E3
Yellow River (Huanghe)
  D3
Yunnan C4

Zhejiang E4

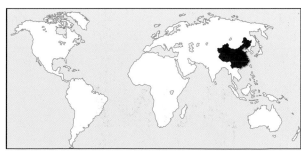

Quick Facts

Official Name   People's Republic of China

Capital   Beijing

Official Language   Putonghua (Mandarin)

Population   1.3 billion

Land Area   9.6 million square kilometres

Provinces   Anhui, Fujian, Gansu, Guangdong, Guizhou, Hainan, Hebei, Heilongjiang, Henan, Hubei, Hunan, Jiangsu, Jiangxi, Jilin, Liaoning, Qinghai, Shaanxi, Shandong, Shanxi, Sichuan, Yunnan, Zhejiang

Highest Point   Zhumulangma Feng (Mt. Everest) (8,843 metres)

Major Rivers   Xi River, Yangtze River, Yellow River

Major Religions   Buddhism, Taoism

Important Festivals   Chinese New Year (Spring Festival), Dragon Boat Festival, Mid-Autumn Festival, Tomb-Sweeping Day

Currency   Renminbi (RMB 10.25= £1 in 2010)

Beautiful flame trees line the banks of a river in China.

Glossary

arid: very dry

calligraphy: a traditional art of elegant writing

classical: describing a style of literature or art that follows certain ancient rules and forms

combat: fighting

Communism: a type of political system in which the entire community or the government owns all property equally

Communist: a person who supports Communism, and based on its laws, does not belong to any social class

Confucius: a Chinese teacher and philosopher who believed in the importance of respecting one's elders and in maintaining peace and order in society

dialect: variety of a language

dynasty: a line of rulers belonging to the same family

embroidery: the art of decorating a piece of cloth with needlework

enforce: to make sure a rule is obeyed or a belief practiced

hongbao: red packets containing money that are given out during Chinese New Year

minority regions: areas of China that are dominated by a minor ethnic group

modernize: to update or make new

monsoon: a season of heavy rain

moon cake: a small, round cake filled with a sweet paste and eaten during the Mid-Autumn Festival

municipality: a big city area that has some power to govern itself

opium: the dried juice of the poppy seed, often used as a drug

opponent: an enemy or a person who disagrees with a set of beliefs

philosopher: a person who seeks knowledge about human behaviour and the meaning of life

plateau: a large, flat area surrounded by lower land

primitive: early

putonghua: the common language

republic: a country where political power rests with the people

reunion: a gathering of relatives or friends after some time apart

revolution: a war in which the people overthrow their leader. A sudden, far-reaching change.

stilt-walker: a person who walks and performs while standing on long sticks

zither: a musical instrument with strings stretched over a board

For More Information

Books

Bojang, Ali Brownlie. *China*. World in Focus series. London: Wayland, 2009

Cotterell, Arthur. *Ancient China*. DK Eyewitness Books series. London: Dorling Kindersley Publishing, 2006

Goodman, Polly. *China*. Food around the World series. London: Wayland, 2010

Morris, Ting. *Ancient China*. Arts and Crafts of the Ancient World series. London: Franklin Watts, 2006

Nash, Deborah. *Made in China*. London: Frances Lincoln Children's Books, 2006

Pirotta, Saviour. *Traditional Stories from China*. London: Wayland, 2006

Ryder, Joanne. *Panda Kindergarten*. London: Collins Publishers, 2009

Zucker, Jonny. *Lanterns and Firecrackers: A Chinese New Year Story*. Festival Time! series. London: Frances Lincoln Children's Books, 2005

DVDs

China: A Century of Revolution. (Zeitgeist Films, 2007).

China Rises: A Documentary in Four Parts. (Discovery Channel, 2008).

Globe Trekker: Ultimate China. (Pilot Productions, 2005).

Websites

www.ancientchinalife.com

A general guide filled with engaging articles on life in ancient China.

www.chinafacttours.com/facts/chinese-legends-and-stories.html

Features a bumper collection of folk tales, stories, myths, and legends that are both entertaining and educational.

www.chinapage.com

This extensive selection of factoids also has audio files showcasing the country's music and language.

www.sacu.org/culture.html

A good source of reference with easy-to-read sections including history, language, traditions, and more.

Note to parents and teachers: Every effort has been made by the Publishers to ensure that these websites are suitable for children, that they are of the highest educational value, and that they contain no inappropriate or offensive material. However, because of the nature of the Internet, it is impossible to guarantee that the contents of these sites will not be altered. We strongly advise that Internet access is supervised by a responsible adult.

Index